Romance
REKINDLED

RICK BUNDSCHUH
DAVE GILBERT

Bob,
    I can love you thru God's love.
                ♡ Nancy
    Happy Valentines Day '90

HARVEST HOUSE PUBLISHERS
Eugene, Oregon 97402

ROMANCE REKINDLED

Copyright © 1988 by Harvest House Publishers
Eugene, Oregon 97402

Library of Congress Catalog Card Number 87-082790
ISBN 0-89081-650-6

Printed in the United States of America.

*With love and thanks
to Debbie Gilbert*

CONTENTS

INTRODUCTION

This book comes from our hearts. It is our belief that romance for married couples has fallen on hard times. What at first came naturally has been snuffed out by the stress of making a living, kids, commitments, and a general feeling of tiredness that comes at the end of a busy day.

Where has the exhilarating feeling of being in love gone? Is there any hope of rekindling those emotions that made falling in love so much fun? To this we answer a resounding YES!

Those feelings can be restored and maintained in a growing marriage. What it takes is a desire to love, a little creativity, and a sense of risk and adventure. The couples that have taken our words seriously and have applied the concepts and ideas we suggest have all told us of new-found sparks in their love for each other. The addition of romance into their marriage has helped them grow closer than either thought possible.

That's why we're so excited to be writing this book. These chapters contain vital information every married couple needs to reignite the embers of their romance. It is our hope that you are encouraged in your marriage. We hope that no matter how cold those embers have grown, this book will act as gasoline and cause you to explode into a romantic fire of love and passion.

Sound impossible? It's not! But there are a few things that you must keep in mind as you read that will help you gain the most benefit.

READ THE WHOLE BOOK—Even though we divided

the book by specific subjects, many of our ideas apply to other areas of concern. You are likely to find ideas in every section that you can use.

HIDE THIS BOOK!—If your spouse thinks you're "trying out ideas" that you read in a book, he or she will not view them quite as romantically. We don't need to be quoted or credited. We want you to get all the credit!

BE CREATIVE—Change our ideas to fit into your style and personality. Our hope is that we will spark an idea in you as you read. Add to the ideas, making them more wild or mellowing them out. Create a date that you have fun on or that's an expression of love that is straight from your heart.

GIVE THIS BOOK AWAY—Buy a copy for someone else's unromantic spouse. Tell them about what a difference you've noticed in your marriage since you've been thinking romantically. Follow up later to see how they've changed.

THINK ROMANCE—When you have a free moment to dream, think about ways you can show your spouse how much you love him or her. Think about what makes him special or what might please her. A true romantic loves to think about love (and not necessarily sex!).

As you can see, this book demands action. It was not written for you to dream about but for you to apply. Act upon the practical advice and ideas you find here. We hope our efforts help you to never lose that "loving feeling."

ROMANCE

*Why
Romance?*

REKINDLED

I love you—mystical words, enchanted words, longed for, hoped for, dreamed about. I love you—words that motivate us, energize us, and make us feel confident because we know that we are loved by our beloved. Romantic love conquers our fears, calms our anxieties, and helps us feel good about ourselves. That kind of love allows us to function at our highest level. Romantic love is good for us.

Romance is essentially enchantment, excitement, passion, and love of one person for another. It is the element which gives poets many of their lines and is the common thread of many a book and film. Romance touches almost every one of us in some form. It is a very pleasant touch. People who say they are "romantics" usually mean that they enjoy having some kind of adventure with the one they love. They usually put great value on things that have little or no value to anyone but themselves and their beloved. Because of this, many see romantic people as silly, starry-eyed optimists living naively in an imaginary world.

But one can have both feet firmly planted on the ground and still know the joys of romance. Those who humbug this aspect of life are missing out on some wonderful benefits.

Romance offers security and validation to the one who is being "romanced." It says: "You are special." "You are loved." "Your thoughts and ideas are important to me." Many special people have never been told how wonderful and special they are by the very people they are special to.

Romance offers excitement within a relationship.

In preparing for our previous book, *Dating Your Mate*, we often gathered groups of people together (oftentimes complete strangers recruited from airport lobbies or parties) and reviewed some of the dating ideas on which we wanted input. The excitement level over the ideas suggested quite surprised us. It seemed that just the idea of something romantic (and different than dinner and the movies) sounded all of the bells in many people.

Romance is exciting and fun. It gives your mind something to look forward to and things to remember. It breaks the monotony that many relationships find themselves in and adds dimension and zest.

Romance gives a tangible expression to a love that we may already have. In many cases, we fail to express to the ones we love the most just how special they are. Romance offers this in the form of a quiet walk along the shore, a meal shared in soft candlelight, or a written expression of our feelings.

Some men have been known to answer their wife's question "Do you love me?" with "Well, I married you didn't I?" People need more from their spouse. They need frequent affirmation. They need to see love demonstrated in a visible way over and over again.

For the person initiating romantic encounters, there is another payoff: the excitement of doing something special (and possibly secret) for your beloved and the burst of creativeness that often comes when we get caught up in doing wonderful things for another person.

Romance also gives us "pegs" to hang memories on. It gives us milestones that we can look back on with warmth and joy. In some ways a richly romantic relationship creates a beautiful history that allows the foundation of love to increase in capacity.

We believe that God created people to be multidimensional. We are physical, social, intellectual, emotional, and spiritual beings. So one good way to draw closer to each other is to develop our spiritual lives. The closer two people draw to God, the closer they are able to draw to each other.

Romance very often leads to a physical display of love. It invites intimacy because it is investing in the life of another person. Not only does romance lead to physical love, but it makes that love more enjoyable, sweeter, and better.

Why then are so many people not experiencing romantic love in their marriages? It is our conclusion that most have fallen into this state of boredom unknowingly and unintentionally. Most couples began their romance with a torrent of emotion. To define it in a word, they were infatuated. Their relationship was based on fantasy, externals. The person was always on their mind—all they wanted to do was please this individual.

Over time the intensity of their initial romantic feelings faded, but unfortunately in many cases the quieter but still-romantic love did not always fill the void. Other things began to fill their minds. The time, creativity, and energy that once was given to their beloved is now spent on pressures at work, money concerns, kids, and things.

Women seem to be more sensitive to this fading of romantic love. Dr. James Dobson says:

> Women yearn to be the special sweethearts of their men, being respected and appreciated and loved with tenderness. This is why a housewife often thinks about her husband during the day and eagerly awaits his arrival home; it explains why their wedding anniversary is more important to her, and why he gets clobbered when he forgets it. It explains why she is constantly reaching for him when he is at home, trying to pull him out of the newspaper or television set; it explains why "Absence of Romantic Love in My Marriage" ranked so high as a source of depression among women, whereas men would have rated it somewhere in the vicinity of last place.

Regardless of whether you are a woman or a man, lack of romantic love in your marriage will affect you. It is our belief that God created the marriage union so that a couple could experience an all-encompassing spiritual, emotional, and physical attraction for each other that would last the rest of their lives. We were meant to live as husband and wife, as one flesh, not as brother and sister.

Maybe you have felt hopeless concerning the possibility of romantic love in your marriage. For one reason or another you have thought "My spouse is just not that type." DON'T BELIEVE IT! We are all emotional beings who desperately need the intimacy that comes from romantic love for our spouse.

It is our hope that this book will challenge you to work on your love. Love can come to you at any age in any stage of your marriage if you are willing to do what is necessary to let it happen. No matter how bad your marriage is right now, you can fall in love with your mate all over again.

Walter Trobisch says about love:

> Love is a feeling to be learned.
> It is tension and fulfillment.
> It is deep longing and hostility.
> It is gladness and it is pain.
> There is not one without the other.
> Happiness is only part of love.
> This is what has to be learned.
> Suffering belongs to love also.
> This is the mystery of love,
>   its beauty and its burden.
> Love is a feeling to be learned.

True romantic love is an unconditional commitment to an imperfect being. Romantic love is more than a warm, tingly feeling; it is a choice that we make. We've found that people who have made the choice to be romantically in love with their mate are happy people who enjoy their lives. The words "I love you" have signaled an end to their search—they've found their life's mate and can be assured they are loved. Our hope is that you've found the security, the peace, and the fun it is to be hopelessly in love with your spouse.

Just for fun, we'd like to challenge you to take the G.B.R.A. (Gilbert-Bundschuh Romance Analysis) to determine the kind of romance quotient you have.

G.B.R.A.

1. When did you last touch each other affectionately?
   A. Today
   B. Yesterday
   C. On the honeymoon
   D. Can't remember

2. When did you last show affection for each other in public?
   A. This week
   B. Last week
   C. Last month
   D. We don't appear together in public

3. When you kiss would your kisses be characterized by your spouse as:
   A. Curls my socks!
   B. With feeling
   C. Perfunctory
   D. Like kissing Grandma

4. Do you feel physically attracted to your mate?
   A. Zowie!
   B. Only have eyes for him/her
   C. After a diet
   D. When we're in the dark

5. How often do you date?
   A. Once a week
   B. Once a month
   C. Once a decade
   D. What's a date?

6. Your spouse would say the dates you go on are:
   A. Creative and fun
   B. Mildly entertaining
   C. Same place, same thing
   D. Few and far between

7. What would your spouse say about your sex life?
   A. Hot!
   B. Could use some improvement, but we have fun
   C. Yawn!
   D. ZZZZZZZZ

8. The last time I gave my wife flowers unexpectedly was:
   A. This month
   B. Last month
   C. When I was courting her
   D. I plan to at her funeral

9. My spouse gets love notes from me:
   A. Frequently
   B. On special occasions
   C. When I want something
   D. I don't put anything in writing

10. My spouse knows I love him/her because:
    A. I show and tell him/her regularly
    B. I tell him/her when I'm in the mood
    C. I married him/her
    D. I'm still married to him/her

Grading Key

4 points for A
3 points for B
2 points for C
1 point for D

35-40	You should have written this book
30-34	A regular Romeo and Juliet
25-29	Carefully read this book
Below 24	Memorize every word in this book

After you have completed this analysis, have your spouse take it. Although the test is hardly scientific, it should be a good indicator of strengths and potential weaknesses in your romantic life together.

Every couple has difficulty keeping one another in the position of importance that each deserves. In the following pages you will find a number of ideas that can help refocus your relationship and rekindle romance. Get ready for excitement!

ROMANCE

*The Wonderful
Difference Between
Men and Women*

REKINDLED

2

For romance to have the best chance for growth and survival, it is very important to realize that there is a distinct difference between what lures, entices, and ignites men and what has the same effect on women.

The sexes do not think the same way nor view the world and the events in it the same way—which, at the very least, makes living together an adventure.

Periodically one sex or the other in our society takes to pointing out the differences or distinctions in a negative way, and for a time there is a flood of books, articles, and cartoons picturing men as passive, weak-willed, noncommittal bores or women as sniveling, nagging wenches. While this kind of literature makes whoever is being pictured in the more "saintly" light feel better, it probably does little to really help the sexes enjoy the differences and make the most out of them.

If romance is what we would like to share with our mate

it is important that we use the right kind of lure. No one uses salmon eggs to entice a mouse or a hunk of cheese to catch a marlin. What perks up the interest of males is distinctly different on many occasions than what sparks a female. We must use the right lures if we want to entice romance.

There are many complex reasons why men and women respond differently but the fact is . . . they do. While there may be some exceptions, it is a general rule that women respond in the following ways.

Women have a tendency to desire things that stroke the emotional strings. They enjoy something that has secret symbolism, they enjoy sentimental gifts, cards, and thoughts. They take great pleasure in things that affirm their specialness. Women tend to enjoy the small details in a romantic setting that add to the atmosphere. In short, many women enjoy an almost imaginary world being created for them.

Women enjoy softness, tenderness, and openness. Women want to feel vital, important, and capable—but they also enjoy the feeling of being protected, cared for, and nurtured.

Most women also enjoy the sensual, physical side of romance but tend to see it as the grand finale after a long, sweet overture.

Women, regardless of how long they have been married, love to be courted. This has to do with not only the immediate message of "You are special and important to me" but also with the sentimental memories that are often connected with courtship.

Most women would prefer to have their spouse initiate dating, special moments, and often even sex. This does not mean that women do not take the role of initiator. They do, but most would prefer to take it occasionally rather than consistently.

Women often put great value in the message behind gifts they receive from their spouse. Because of this, many times they are disappointed when they receive what they consider a "utility" item (such as a vacuum cleaner or cookware) as a birthday or anniversary gift . . . even if the item cost a small fortune. What women generally look for in a surprise or gift is the tender feeling and indication of their uniqueness—not the practicality.

What men are often looking for in romance is not on the surface as easily defined as for women. Men have been taught to be much more guarded about their sentimentality than have women. Most men do thoroughly enjoy being with someone with whom they can share their feelings and still be respected.

Men enjoy the sensual part of romance. They enjoy the sight of their spouse "dressed to kill." They enjoy the trace of a woman's perfume. They enjoy the feeling of being desirable. To build up a man's expectations with a warm and romantic evening only to end the night with a quick kiss good night or by falling asleep can mean big trouble in the morning.

Men are often more pragmatic in their approach to romance than women are (which is why it is generally a waste to buy flowers for a man . . . he may say to himself "What am I supposed to do with these?"). Gifts and special things for men can be of a far more practical variety, but men still value knowing that they are loved and cared about by their spouse.

It is often expected that a man should learn to be sensitive, romantic, and sentimental... or in other words that he should learn to think about what is exciting and romantic to a woman. But a wife who truly wants to experience the full spectrum of a romantic relationship should be prepared to discover the kind of activities that make up romance in a man's world.

Men often enjoy active and adventurous "dates" that may, to a woman, seem far-removed from the perfume-and-lace idea of romance. To romance a man may mean hitting the river with him on a raft, sleeping in tents, battling bugs and broken fingernails. It may mean doing things together that are part of a man's world.

Certainly it is fair if we ask men to learn "softness and tenderness" that we ask women to discover a bit of "hardiness and adventure."

Not all men are the rugged outdoor type, but all men consider it wonderfully exciting if their spouse attempts to have a place in their world. If a woman is interested in things that interest her man, a bond of affirmation and love is created. To a man, a woman who loves the things he loves sets the stage for a romantic relationship.

Men enjoy occasional pampering and attention. They enjoy messages that focus on their ego or hold them in esteem and respect. A basic difference between the sexes is that men find their worth in being respected while what is most important to a woman is to be cherished and loved.

Men need praise. Most men enjoy seeing that their effort at romance is producing joy or excitement for their wife. They enjoy the feeling that they are doing a good job of being a loving husband.

Men even enjoy being pursued and seduced occasionally. While this is not the usual case, sometimes a man needs a woman to show him what he really needs. During times of stress, most men become totally occupied with the problems that cause the tension. The sex drive is diminished, when what he needs most is the loving caress of his wife. Romance becomes all the more exciting when a man and a woman learn what makes the other person feel the "tingles" and then lovingly put it into use.

The following are ideas that have been broken down into two categories. One includes those ideas that most likely would be of interest to women; and the other, those ideas which would most likely be of interest to men.

IDEAS THAT MEN MAY ENJOY

An Adventure Date

What has your husband always wanted you to do with him? Go hunting? River rafting? Skydiving? Hang gliding? Go ahead—do it with him! Before you go you may need to prepare yourself by getting some professional lessons, but your interest can pay big dividends.

King for a Day

This is a day just devoted to him. If he likes you to fan him and feed him grapes, then this is the day to do it. Make him feel like a king. Who knows—he may give you one of these days in return!

Rent a Jeep

Rent a jeep for your man and spend the day off-roading. Make sure to pack a big lunch and screw the lids down tight!

The Car Show

Treat your spouse to a custom car or boat show. Learn as much as you can from him about the various kinds of cars, engines, paint jobs, etc.

A Camping Trip

Plan a camping trip just for the two of you. Make reservations and obtain permits if you are going to be in areas that require them. Plan on carrying your share of the weight and get used to dehydrated food if you are going to hike into your destination site.

Target Shooting

Ask your husband to take you target shooting. Blast away all day at skeet targets, bull's-eyes, or bottles. Bring a lunch for a break in the blazing bullets.

Macho Man Movie Night

Rent a bunch of movies that appeal to your spouse— John Wayne, Rocky, war movies, sci-fi, to name a few.

Cook up a batch of popcorn and try not to cover your eyes.

The Fights

Go with your man to the fights or a wrestling match. Learn to shout and cheer (be as convincing as possible). Bet your spouse an ice cream on the outcome of the fight.

Computer Games for Two

If your husband is a computer buff, surprise him with games that he can play on the computer... providing he plays with you. Establish a penalty for the one with the least points at the end of play. (For example: Loser must scratch winner's back for five minutes.)

IDEAS ESPECIALLY TO PLEASE A WOMAN

The Nail Job

Surprise your wife by taking her out for a manicure at a fashionable salon. Wait patiently while she is getting her nails done or go shopping for a nice bracelet to set off those beautiful nails.

The Chocolate Bar

Take your wife to a chocolate bar (like a salad bar, only it features all chocolate goodies... these are found in many cities) or create one for her. (You can always substitute whatever appeals to your woman—for example, an exotic fruit bar.)

Rent a Romance

Bring home a load of musicals, romance films ("Gone with the Wind," "Romeo and Juliet," "Somewhere in Time," etc.), or whatever else your spouse would enjoy seeing. Whip up popcorn and beverages—and make sure to have a box of Kleenex handy.

Art Museum Day

Take your wife to a museum of her choice. Patiently walk with her through the exhibits looking as long as she wants to look. Buy her a memento from the gift shop to remember the day by or find a print of a painting she liked in a local print shop, have it framed, and give it to her as a gift a little later.

The Flower Mart

Give your beloved a trip to the flower mart and enough money to turn your home into springtime. Wander through the stalls of flowers and try and learn the names of a few.

Crafts Fair

Take your wife to a local crafts fair. The two of you wander around the booths together and eat goodies at the concession stand.

If your spouse sees something she really wants, you can always pick up the artist's card and special-order it as a surprise later on.

Model Home Tours

Take your spouse on an inexpensive tour through model homes. Check out the interior design of each one and vote for the rooms you like the best. Try and hit a few housing divisions and then top things off with a nice dinner out.

Fashion Show

Take your wife to a fashion show. Let her get excited about the designs shown. After the show give her some money to go shopping for fashions at the mall. (Go with her, of course, and applaud as she models.)

Class Act

Enroll with your wife in a night class that she is interested in. Learn with her as much as you can and be a support. Plan to eat out on the nights there are classes.

ROMANCE

How to Help
an Unromantic Spouse
Discover Romance

REKINDLED

3

In many relationships there seems to be one partner (and not always the woman) who is the "hopeless romantic" while the other seems not to have a romantic bone in his or her body.

The background, temperament, and current stress situation all contribute to making some people far more unresponsive or unromantic than their mates would have hoped for. But even for the most reluctant of personalities, romance can be awakened. The person may never quite act like the Prince Charming or sultry siren that their spouse may wish for, but he or she can certainly come closer to the romantic heartbeat than before.

The romantic spouse is never to concentrate his effort on "What can I do to make my dud of a mate more romantic?" but on "What romantic thing can I do for this person I love?" The very minute we pin an expectation to our romantic actions, we are waiting to disappoint ourselves. Loving and romantic actions must be given simply because of love for the spouse, not in order to get some sort of reward as a payback.

If a person feels the pressure to act romantic, he often will revolt and become even less responsive. (The temptation to throw this book at your spouse and say "Why can't you be more romantic?" is likely to be greeted with as much enthusiasm as a cold shower.) Romance should never be used as a trick to get the other person in a position of indebtedness.

The road to warming up an unresponsive spouse is often a long one and the progress sometimes becomes difficult to measure. But with effort and perseverance, the enthusiasm of love can be infectious. Reward each step of the way with positive reinforcement. Responding in an exciting and appreciative way to any romantic gesture can be a great motivator for having the action repeated.

Besides avoiding expectations, there are a few other key ideas that can help to dislodge a complacent lover into participation in the excitement of the relationship.

Consider the timing. Be very sensitive to the levels of stress and fatigue that your spouse may be experiencing. If he has had a hard or difficult week, he needs to relax on a date. Conversely, if life has been a little dull, he may need adventure.

Try to avoid a conflict between the romantic idea that you have set in motion and some important deadline or meeting. For example, it may not be wise to force your spouse to choose between doing something new and a little exotic with you and watching the final play-off of this season's football teams. You may lose. Your spouse may feel guilty. Both of you may become angry.

Compete favorably with other events. This is especially important when you are first initiating dates or activities that cause you to spend intimate time together. Whatever it is that you would like to sell your mate on doing should have more interest than the TV program she may have to miss or the nap he may have to forfeit. A solution to this is to try and build your initial dates around something that your spouse likes to do. For example, rather than watch a TV football game you may surprise your spouse with tickets to a live game in a neighboring city, complete with hotel rooms for the weekend. Sure, you may spend a Saturday in the stands, but you will have the rest of the weekend with him all to yourself.

Decide what your spouse needs right now. Be sensitive. Ask God for wisdom. Ask yourself: What would be appreciated—time alone or with a crowd, something relaxing or something adventurous, something you have done before or something new, time to talk or time to be entertained?

Don't use overkill. If your relationship has been fairly dull and routine, to suddenly deluge your spouse with love notes and dates may cause shock or suspicion... regardless of what you say. "Okay, what did you do to the car?" or "Dear, is there something that you need to tell me about?" may be the responses you receive to your sudden gestures of love. Slowly turn up the heat so that the relationship boils over gradually.

Learn the use of affirmation. People, as did Pavlov's famous dog, respond much better to rewards than they do to stinging barbs. By noticing (not necessarily gushing over) any act of love and commenting about it, we increase the odds of it happening again! Comments like "I bet you didn't know that I always feel so loved by you when you open the door for me" are ways of verbalizing the positive things we feel and possibly continuing and expanding loving behavior.

A note of caution is important here. If you are hoping to awaken your mate's interest in romance, a classic no-no to avoid is comparison. Once a spouse starts the "Why can't you be like so-and-so?" the battle is lost.

Put things in writing. As corny as it may sound, a red-hot love note can prepare a mind for romance. It also can be read and reread anytime an extra jolt is needed. Love notes make great keepsakes as well.

With common sense and wise use of the tips given, even an entrenched anti-romantic can thaw. (Of course, the longer they have been in the freezer the slower the thaw.) For some gentle ideas of what to do to spark some excitement in your spouse, consider trying one of the following.

Refinish Together

Make a simple date out of going to a garage sale, buying a piece of furniture that you both like, and then refinishing it together. This kind of joint project, while not as glamorous as going out on the town, can provide a sense of togetherness... and you have something to show for it at the same time.

Dress Differently

One way to wake up your spouse is to start dressing up more. Wear nicer clothes, wear cologne or perfume, begin an exercise program and perhaps lose weight. Oftentimes a spouse will notice these differences that occur and be motivated to change as well, or at least have a renewed interest.

Create a Pamper Day

Select one day to pamper your mate with all the attention and special little "perks" you can dream up. Do this as a secret, or announce your intentions in a card the morning of Pamper Day. You can even make this a regular event by selecting one day a month to be Pamper Day for your beloved.

Out of the Hat

Think of all of the things that your spouse likes to do, eat, read, watch, etc. Write down as many ideas for those things as you can on slips of paper. (For example: Go out to a restaurant for a piece of strawberry pie.)

Dump all of the papers in a hat and tell your mate that you want to do something special for him that evening. Ask him to select an idea out of the hat and then make plans to do it.

Collectable Companion

If your mate likes to collect anything from doorknobs to

back scratchers, suggest that you would like to go on a hunt for the items. Make a weekend of it by going to new fields of exploration. Or if you hear of a special collectors' show, make plans to present the trip as a surprise.

ROMANCE

*The Work
of Romance*

REKINDLED

4

"You get what you pay for." Many of us have repeated that old proverb to our friends, employees, and family members. But the old saying is never more true than when it comes to romance. To be romantic is not natural for most people. It is a learned skill. It takes thought, planning, insight, time, motivation, and effort. These are the true "costs" of romancing your spouse. (Many very romantic gestures cost little money or nothing at all.)

Each and every one of us can have a warmly romantic relationship if we are willing to put out the effort that it takes to create one.

Since we all have the same 24 hours in a day, and most of us find almost all of those hours occupied with "important" things, creating a romantic life means some re-adjustments.

The presence or absence of high-quality romance can be traced to the proper management of two factors: our priorities and our personal discipline (or lack of it).

Our real priorities in life (not necessarily our expressed priorities) can be judged accurately by the things in which we invest the most time.

Some of the hardest work of romance comes from having to evaluate and make changes in the priorities we hold in order to put the interests and time our spouse needs at the top of the pile.

The hard work of romance comes in creating and guarding time for special moments when there are so many other demands that continually call out to us. The hard work comes in clearing our mind of other thoughts and meditating on our beloved.

Once we have set aside special time to spend with our spouse, it takes hard work to make sure we do not allow laziness to overtake us and spend those special hours plopped in front of the TV. Romantic love takes disciplined effort in order to be creative, thoughtful, and exciting.

Some helpful hints to begin the hard work of romantic love:

Develop an eye for intimate details. These are the little quirks, likes, dislikes, seldom-mentioned desires, and customs that almost every person has. It really comes down to knowing your beloved and paying attention to what he or she does and thinks.

For example, a romantic lover usually will know things like the kind of perfume his wife wears, her shoe size, color preference, musical tastes, the hobbies or crafts that interest her and some of the details about these, the books she enjoys, the kind of films she prefers to see. These little details allow the spouse to know what interests his mate and to be able to share in the little intimacies that make that person special. (For help in this area, see the chart at the end of this chapter.)

Make the effort to control the events in life rather than merely allowing them to happen. This is especially true when it comes to romantic evenings out. It is far more desirable to have an evening planned in advance secretly than it is to stand around the kitchen trying to decide where to go at the last minute.

Some helpful steps are to get a calendar and block out a night a week where you will do something with your beloved. Make sure to allow nothing to interfere with those plans. Call NOW for a baby-sitter—not the night before. Examine your budget to know your "range" and plan accordingly.

Create a personal calendar that you keep in your office or purse. On it mark out special days on which you plan to do something for the one you love. For example, one week send flowers for no reason other than because you love her. Another week bring home a quart of his favorite ice cream with a love note. A different week plan to write a love letter or send a card. Something special as infrequently as once a month goes a long way toward a romantic relationship.

Take a lunch hour once a week to devote to your spouse. (In some cases this may mean you'll have to eat on the run.) This can include such things as taking him or her out to lunch, bringing a specially prepared meal to him at the office or job site (take the lunch he brought and save it for tomorrow). It can mean going to a mall and buying a little something to surprise your wife with or shopping for cards that say what your heart feels.

You can even take a lunch hour and sneak home or into your mate's car and hang love notes all over the place.

Plan a vacation designed for romance! Take your spouse to someplace you have never been before. Oftentimes good information about places and events far and near can be found in magazines like *Sunset, Bride's Magazine,* or regional magazines (which most major cities or areas have) and the travel section of the newspaper.

To get good rates and information you will have to plan ahead and correspond. If you want to keep the destination a surprise, have all of the brochures sent to your office or a friend's home.

On the following page is a chart that you can complete and keep as a reference to take with you when shopping for your spouse.

Clothes or dress size _____

Waist size _____

Shoe size _____

Bra size _____

Neck size _____

Color preference _____

Brand preference _____

Perfume or cologne preference _____

Favorite gemstone _____

Favorite music _____ performer _____

Special song _____

Hobbies, crafts, or sports information _____

Favorite books or authors _____

Favorite foods _____

Favorite restaurants _____

Favorite flavor of ice cream _____

Favorite kind of sweets _____

Favorite place to visit _____

Favorite film or director _____

Favorite thing to say _____

Birthdate _____

Anniversary date _____

Other important dates to remember _____

_____

ROMANCE

*Setting
the Mood*

REKINDLED

5

You only have to spend a few minutes in Disneyland to understand the importance of setting the mood for romance to begin. The magic kingdom is built largely around an environment especially designed to shift you from the world outside the park (with its parking lots, traffic, and competing architecture of every fast-food joint) to a world that Disney created. Every section of the theme park shifts your mood, from the homeyness of Main Street to the slick look of Tomorrowland. All of the workers appear in costume and act in character to contribute toward a very enjoyable experience in a world that has been created for you. A world, by the way, that takes a great deal of expense and energy to maintain.

Romance works in somewhat the same way. It is greatly helped by the right kind of environment. Rare are the spontaneous times when the right conditions (atmosphere, mood, desire, etc.) all come together. If we sit around waiting for the right conditions to fall together magically, we may be waiting a long time!

Most of the time an atmosphere where romance can bloom takes planning and thought.

A good setup is important for several reasons. It tells your mate "I care enough to take time for you" or "I notice the little details that you like...which means I'm thinking especially about you." These are the unspoken love notes of setting a romantic environment.

Setting the mood also plays with us emotionally. It prepares us to enjoy, open up, relax, and refocus on the beloved. Particularly for a woman, the mood strikes a warm chord deep inside. It prepares a couple for closeness, dialogue, and even physical intimacy.

For the most part, a mood must be created. It doesn't just sprout up from nowhere (only weeds in the garden and fleas on the dog do this). It must be planned and executed. This takes work...but the rewards are delightful!

There are a number of areas that we can work on to provide the optimum romantic setup. Although we may not be able to get all of them completely polished, anything we can do contributes toward the excitement of time together.

Moods are often set early in the day. A tone can be set in how we wake up our spouse, how breakfast progresses, and the way a couple parts company in the morning. As hard as a cheerful beginning is to produce some mornings, often it will contribute toward a cheerful ending of the day.

One important area of the setup is the actual physical environment in which your beloved and you will spend your time. A key idea is to change the location from what you are used to. For example, if you live in the country you may want to go to the city. If you live in the city, the country may offer a new and romantic setting. Anything that changes from the usual can stimulate romance.

Proper use of lighting adds dimension to romance. Candles are far more mood-setting than fluorescent lights, dim lights are far more sensual than carnival lighting.

You can add a dimming switch to your house and control the environment of your own home by dimming the lights to a golden dusk whenever you would like to set a gentle, romantic mood. (For real fun, put a dimmer switch in without your spouse's knowledge and turn down the lights one night for an evening of home romance.)

Music is a natural part of any romantic environment. Select the kind of music that you think would be of interest to your spouse and play it softly in the background. Music has a way of bringing back memories, so you may wish to select something that is a special song between the two of you or an altogether new or unpredictable piece that will, each time it is played again, remind your beloved of the warm and delightful evening that you are enjoying right now. This is simply using music to create great memories for the future.

Whether inside or out, a lightly dancing fire is wildly romantic to many people. Spread out blankets on the living room floor and enjoy each other's companionship in the warm glow of the fireplace.

For romantic evenings at home, simple things like a clean and vacuumed house add a great deal to any kind of romance taking place. The same is true of an unplugged phone. (If your spouse is a business person, you may want to do this on the sly. This move may decrease profits, but it sure can profit your marriage.) Farming the kids out or occupying them with all three of the Star Wars videos and a trash-can-size container of popcorn may help limit interference.

On your next stay at a hotel, collect a few DO NOT DISTURB signs and put them on the doorknobs to gently let the neighbors know that this is not the best time to borrow a cup of sugar.

On some special occasions you may even want to remove the clocks so that time is irrelevant.

Keep an eye out for details that will help build the atmosphere of love. Use a cloth table cover (go out and buy one if you have to), cloth napkins, and clever napkin holders. The nicest dishes and silverware you have are little marks that say "You mean the world to me."

A room full of flowers adds an aura of enchantment that few other things can. Make a stop at the flower market and load up on the kinds of flowers that will help produce a visual and scented message of love.

If a meal is part of the romantic evening, try and postpone cleanup until later (like the next day) or hire a neighbor kid to come in and tidy up for you.

With a little extra thought, meals can be fun and delightfully romantic!

Make use of the natural beauty that surrounds us all. Sunsets, full moons, gentle rainfall, falling snow, or even crashing thunderstorms can be celebrated as an excuse for romance. Mountain peaks, streambeds, or the top of a cliff can make wonderful backdrops for love.

If your romantic time together is outdoors, make sure to make it comfortable for your spouse. If it may be hot, bring shade. If cold, make sure to pack extra blankets or jackets.

If you are going out on the town, try and select places where the environment is designed for romance. The corner family pizza joint may not provide the kind of ambience you are looking for.

Small details are like pluses or minuses that can tip the scale for creating a mood of romance that works or that fizzles. For example, making sure that the car you are going out in is clean and vacuumed (old french fries off the seat and wrappers picked up). You may even want to buy a special tape to play for the evening and slip it into the tape deck beforehand. (Make sure to tell your spouse why you bought it.) On your way to your destination, take a different or scenic route: Drive around the harbor or along the back roads. Take your time—make the trip there *part* of the experience and atmosphere!

To really set a mood, make sure that you are dressed for the occasion. Fresh smelling, sharply outfitted and, if you expect the evening to end with a delightful time in the bedroom, you may want to be wearing something new and daring to bed (or buy your mate a goodnight gift of new lingerie).

For a gentle scent throughout your whole house, put a little bit of cologne on your light bulbs when they are cold. As they warm, the scent will be wafting gradually through the house.

The right kind of environment takes time to prepare. It

takes thought. Nothing can squash a well-intentioned evening more than having to rush around doing last-minute details. If you have children, try getting a babysitter well in advance so that you can concentrate on your own preparation and then on giving attention to your spouse. If you go out, rather than rush through dinner to try and make the movie, try limiting what you do that evening to one particular thing... and give yourself plenty of time to enjoy the activity and each other more intimately. Unwind at home rather than coming home to collapse.

Along with the mood-setters suggested, the following ideas are those that can help you set a mood or environment that will be excitingly romantic. Use these or create your own romance for your beloved!

The Bubble Bath

Without your wife knowing, prepare a luxurious bubble bath for her to relax and soak in. You may want to visit your local bath shop and select a fragrant bubble bath. Set up the bathroom with a portable tape deck playing relaxing music, fresh towels, a liberal variety of reading material (stop by the store and pick up a magazine or two your spouse enjoys), and some beverage to sip on. Pull this one during a time when your wife needs to take a few minutes to completely relax.

Time your surprise so that the bathwater is nice and warm by having your wife call you just before she leaves for home from the office or the store. Use soft lighting or candlelight to add to the effect.

Note: Be careful not to sit too close to the edge of the tub. There is a good chance that your spouse may decide to pull you in.

Fireside Chats

Create a mood in your own living room by starting a fire, turning the music on and the lights off. Prepare a tray of goodies to eat and drink. Then cuddle and talk with your spouse next to the fire (or relax in each other's arms and be hypnotized by the flames).

Borrow a Mood

Borrow the use of a friend's house that has an unusual view or location. (You may want to pay for their way out for the evening.) Bring your food with you, spread a blanket on the floor, and enjoy the view over an indoor picnic.

Thunder Thrills

The next time there's a radical lightning storm or thunderstorm, turn off all the lights in your house, open one of the windows, and cuddle together watching the hostile weather. For extra fun, kiss each other when you see a flash of lightning and don't part until you hear the thunder. (This activity is not recommended during tornadoes, tidal waves, or earthquakes.)

Moon Walk

Take your spouse on a leisurely walk during a full

moon. You do not have to go far—just around the neigh-
borhood. Spend your time checking out the moonglow.

Portable Mood

Sometimes it may not be possible to create a mood in
your home (particularly during remodeling). In these
cases, take a drive to some beautiful spot such as a bluff,
the sea shore, the woods, or the top of a downtown
parking lot. Bring a meal with you, flatten the rear seats,
and spread the fixings out on a tablecloth. Slip in a tape of
romantic music and enjoy a meal in the privacy of your
own car.

The Camp Fire

Go to the beach, woods, or a park and build a camp
fire. (Make sure to bring dry wood, matches, and kindling.) Grab a couple of folding chairs and sit together
staring at the flames and making small talk. You may want
to pack some hot chocolate in a thermos for something to
sip on as you spend the night (put the tent and sleeping
bags in the trunk) . . . and remember, only you can prevent
forest fires.

A View in Advance

Go to a nice spot in advance and set up a tent or tarp.
Drive home and load up your car with anything you will
need for a nice, quiet meal together. Make sure to include
things to enhance the atmosphere such as a portable tape
deck, candles, etc.

Try to have the meal prepared in advance and bring a card table, chairs, and tablecloth or simply a blanket to sit on.

Surprise your spouse by picking him or her up at home or work. Take a slow, scenic drive to the place you have already staked out. Note: You may want to throw a couple of sleeping bags in the trunk in case this turns into an all-nighter.

Satin Sheets

Surprise your spouse by purchasing satin sheets and secretly placing them on your bed. Plan a romantic evening and, as the finishing touch, peel back the covers.

Springtime Flower Hunt

There is something wonderful and romantic about springtime. Try taking your beloved on a walk through a field of wildflowers. Collect a bunch for your home and save a few to press in your memory book.

Magic Housecleaning

Take off work early and super clean the house for your wife (or hire someone to do it). There is nothing quite as mood-lifting as thinking you are coming home to a disaster and finding that the house has magically cleaned itself.

Nature Trot

Take a relaxing ride together on horseback through the woods or meadows.

Stargazers

Get a map of the constellations and see how many stars you can locate. (If you live in the city, take a drive to the country for the purpose of stargazing.) Pick several stars that you can easily find again and rename them yourselves.

Fiesta House

Set a fun-filled mood by decorating your house with the theme of a special dinner you have prepared. For example, if you are cooking a Mexican dish you could decorate the house to look like a fiesta had just hit town. Play mariachi music in the background.

Walkin' in the Rain

The next time it really comes down in buckets, put on your galoshes and sweater and take a hike in the rain and share the umbrella. When you come home, fix a big mug of a warm beverage.

ROMANCE

*Listening and
Communicating
with Your Heart*

REKINDLED

6

Romance can flourish in an environment of listening and communication. The problem is that most couples spend far too little time developing this skill. According to a Nielsen study, the average American home has the television on almost seven hours a day. Meanwhile, according to another study, an average married couple talks meaningfully with each other only 20 minutes a week! Perhaps a solution to the lack of romantic love between married couples is to turn off the TV and talk to each other!

Talking to each other means more than "Did you feed the cat today?" or "Please put gas in the car tomorrow." It means two people sharing their thoughts and feelings about a wide range of interests. Good "talking" is the sharing of your heart with your most intimate friend. If a couple started talking like that for 20 minutes a day, their weekly total would be seven times the national average!

Like most of the suggestions made in this book, it pays to begin slowly. For instance, when a husband hears his wife say "Let's talk," a twinge of fear goes through his body. He immediately thinks back to long, drawn-out talks about depressing subjects that went way into the night. Instead of looking forward to a time with his wife to share intimate dreams and heartfelt concerns, he sees it as something to be avoided.

Win the right to be heard. Really listen to what your spouse has to say. Make times in your day to listen that are convenient to the other person. (Don't try to pull him away from Monday night football to talk, or initiate conversation when the kids are screaming. That might fit into your schedule, but not into his.) Remember: Don't expect to change your communication patterns overnight. Listening and communicating with your hearts is something you develop together—it takes time. This kind of intimacy makes it comfortable to share burdens together, to pray together without awkwardness, and to stimulate each other to grow spiritually.

Here are some suggestions that may help you in your desire to communicate better with one another.

1. Studies have shown that the first four minutes you spend together after a time apart (even just a few hours) sets the mood for the time you have together. This "four-minute rule" is worth remembering. How many times have you just greeted your spouse with some unintelligible grunts and gone about your tasks? Take those first four minutes to talk and listen to each other. Share

something that has happened or a thought that came to you. Keep it upbeat as much as possible.

2. When you come home, be ready to greet your spouse. Leave behind the anxiety, fears, and angry feelings that your workday might have produced. One man we know drives over a bridge between his home and work. Each day he makes a conscious decision to leave his work problems at the end of the bridge. The next morning he picks them back up at that same place. Having the right mind-set when you come home is important to good listening.

3. Communicate openly. In a good marriage there is nothing the couple can't talk about. They are free to share their heart without the fear of judgment. They talk about their likes and dislikes, their fears and their dreams, all in an atmosphere of love and intimate trust.

A word of caution here: Be sensitive. Don't talk about subjects that you know will upset your spouse if he or she is exhausted, sick, or in pain. Wait for a better time.

4. Listen carefully. When your spouse is talking, give your total attention. Reading the newspaper or watching TV while your spouse is trying to say something to you sends the message that you don't care.

Listen actively. Nods of the head as well as verbal responses let your spouse know you are listening carefully to what's being said. Look him in the eyes when he's speaking. Repeat back occasionally what you hear her saying to be sure you're interpreting what she means correctly.

5. Make sure you say what you're thinking. Your spouse cannot read your mind, so don't expect him to. Many conflicts and hurt feelings could be avoided if what was on a person's mind had just been expressed. The words "but you should have known" are not fair if what should have been known was never verbally expressed.

6. Touch each other when you talk. A message has three parts. Seven percent is the content of the message. Thirty-eight percent is the tone of voice the message is spoken in. Fifty-five percent is non-verbal, the body language that accompanies the message. Saying "I love you" in a gruff voice while turning away is simply not believable.

The most effective body language is a touch. In a recent study at UCLA, it was found that just to maintain emotional and physical health, men and women need eight to ten meaningful touches each day. This study estimated that if some "type A driven" men would hug their wives several times each day, it would increase their life span by almost two years! (Besides that, think how it would improve their marriages.)

Even the smallest act of touch can help you communicate love and acceptance. Next time you sit down with your spouse to talk, touch them. We think you'll enjoy it.

7. Praise your beloved. Recognize the good in your spouse. Let them know what a great lover you think they are. Make sure you tell them how fortunate you feel that

they married you. If it's sincerely from your heart, recognition and praise gives your spouse's self-worth a boost. It also opens the door for receiving constructive suggestions.

Occasionally we will find a couple that knows each other so well they can communicate volumes to one another without saying a word. In fact, they can be sitting on opposite sides of the room and still know how the other is feeling physically, how they are receiving what is being said by the speaker, how they are feeling toward them, as well as a variety of other information.

This couple has gained a sixth sense through years of good communication. After years of sharing their innermost thoughts and dreams with one another, they now know each other.

Conversation Starters

The dates in this book are designed to further romance. A large part of a romantic relationship is the ability to talk about what you feel and think. But how do you get a conversation going or keep it going? Here is a list of a few questions that might "prime the pump" and help you begin talking from the heart.

Naturally these conversation starters are best used for no other motive than trying to hear and understand the one you love. Keep in mind to set the mood and make conversation a joy, not a job.

- What problem would you gladly pay one-third of all you make this year to see disappear?

- How much would you honestly want to make a year?

- Would too much ruin us?

- What problems would go away if we had as much money as we wanted?

- Who are your five closest friends? Why?

- What do you want your gravestone to read? Why?

- What have you accomplished so far in your life that you are most proud of?

- What do you need to accomplish before you die?

- What is the single biggest need the world has now?

- What would make you cry or become very angry if you saw it happen right now?*

- If you had all the money that you could use, what would you do with your time?

---

*Taken from *The Art of Asking* by Bobb Biehl, © 1981 by Masterplanning Group International, Laguna Niguel, Calif. Used by permission of the author and publisher.

- What one tradition did you have in your home that you would like to continue in ours?

- What one thing you own best represents your life right now?

- What is the funniest thing that you have ever seen happen?

- Who have been the three most important men/women in your life?

- What is the best news you've received?

- When you were a child, what one thing did you want to do when you grew up?

- When you were in high school, what did you like the most about your body? The least?

- What three qualities do you most value in a friend?

- If you had to put a tattoo on your body, where would you put it and what would it say or look like?

- What would you like to pass on to your children after you die?

- What is your favorite holiday?

- If you could change one thing in our relationship in the past, what would it be?

- Who is the most difficult person in your life right now?

- If there were a fire and you could grab one thing from the house, what would it be?

- Which year of your life would you say has been the best so far?

- What has been the greatest adventure of your life so far? What adventure would you still want to go on?**

- What is your favorite room in the house?

- Where did you have the most fun on vacation?

Many dates that couples go on don't do much to help them listen and communicate what is on their heart. The following are some date ideas specifically designed to help a couple get started in this crucial area.

Parking

That's right, just like when you were in high school! Find a romantic view in your car and neck! Some great communicating can go on in a setting like this.

**Taken from *The Serendipity Bible Study Book*, edited by Lyman Coleman, Denny Rydberg, Richard Pease, and Gary Christopherson, © 1986 by Serendipity House, Littleton, Colo. Used by permission of Zondervan Publishing House.

Classical Tunes

Put on your favorite classical music. Sit quietly and listen for awhile. Later, explain to your spouse what you were thinking about during that time. Spread pillows on the floor and share your impressions of the music and the imagery it brought to your mind.

Three Wishes

Create a game out of the old idea of being granted three wishes. Put limitations on the wishes or make them for specific areas such as: three places I wish I could visit, three things under $50 I wish I could get, three people I would like to go and visit. Listen carefully to the wishes of your spouse. Who knows—maybe you can make wishes come true!

ROMANCE

*Putting
Romance
on Paper*

REKINDLED

7

One of the lost arts in our high-tech, fast-paced culture has been the skill of putting in writing what we really feel and think about our beloved—the love letter.

The big difference between an expression of love given in person (or over the phone) as compared to one in writing is that a written expression "goes on giving." Words on paper can be read, cherished, reread, framed, or hidden away with the pressed flowers, locks of hair, and other mementos. A phone call or conversation loses its passion and voice as soon as the communication is over. A letter can be savored, studied, even held. Love letters can be footprints of our love for our spouse. They can track our passion through the years.

You do not have to be a poet or a skilled writer to create a love note to your spouse. The one you love probably knows you well enough not to be bothered with misspellings or poor punctuation. You need not write pages of manuscript to express your love in a meaningful way. One simple sentence can do it!

There are plenty of helps around for those who need a vehicle by which to send their message. Card shops have a widely varying selection of messages and notes that can brighten up any spouse's day.

When using store-bought cards, the best idea is to select the brands that are blank on the inside, allowing you to write your own message. When sending a message card, always be sure to include some of your own ideas, even if you think that the card says it all for you. Your spouse has no way of knowing if the printed message is really yours or Hallmark's unless you affirm it with a line or two of your own.

For the highest kind of romance, always write or print in your own hand. A love letter done on a word processor has about as much appeal as a Christmas newsletter. For an even more romantic effect, purchase high-quality paper and a bottle of colored ink (available at most art stores) and use a fountain pen or a hand-dip lettering pen to write your message. To go all the way, hold the edge of your letter next to a flame to brown or "antique" the edges and seal the envelope with sealing wax.

If your letters are likely to be read by other people before they get to you (or if you have a nosy mother-in-law), you can develop secret code words that only the two of you know the meaning of. In fact, this can turn into quite a game and can be done just for fun.

Writing a good love letter takes time because you must think of the right words to say. People who have a problem with this can find a great deal of help by using a thesaurus.

A love letter is delightful because it says "commitment." It is put down on paper forever. The courage to make those commitments and affirm them is what being married lovers is all about.

Love letters do not have to be all words. With even the most rudimentary skill at doodling, you can create simple little pictures of love with any caption you can design.

Love letters can be all-out efforts as well as mini-notes. A trip to the library and a few readings of the master poets of the "Romantic Age" can help fuel the imagination. Check out how the apostle Paul describes love in chapter 13 of 1 Corinthians. . . . This is a word picture of love that cannot be topped!

Imagine the surprise of any spouse who unexpectedly receives a five-page letter telling them how much they are loved and how special they are. For many, this kind of gift would outweigh anything that money could buy! Gifts of written expression have all of the elements that are so important in a world starved for the personal touch: They take time, thought, intimacy, commitment, effort, and they are tangible . . . they can be handled!

The following ideas can help spark creativity when it comes to communicating in writing.

Pillow Talk

Leave a romantic love note under the pillow. If you're afraid he or she might not find it, pin it on top of the pillow. Some unexpected words of romance written on a scented piece of paper go a long way toward creating a romantic mood that night.

Extended Valentine's Day

This Valentine's Day give her a card that will last all year. Design a card that has fun coupons in it that can be redeemed on the fourteenth of every month. For example, on March 14th give her a two-hour back massage. On April 14th you'll be her slave and do anything she wants you to do all day. Be creative and fun in deciding what to give her each month. This is a card that keeps on giving!

Cardsmith

Keep a supply of card-making supplies stocked in your office and home. When you feel creative, write down your feelings about your spouse in the form of a card. Use stickers, draw stick figures, or cut out a picture from a magazine. A spontaneous handmade card is evidence of your deep love and desire.

Technicolor Picture Puzzle

Many photo-developing places offer the option of putting a photo on a stiff backing and having it cut up like a jigsaw puzzle. The possibilities of how to use this are endless. An example might be that you take a picture of yourself in front of a really special restaurant that you plan to take her out to. Send a puzzle piece a day to her at her workplace or at home until she is able to figure out where you are going on your date.

Acrostic Love Note

Try making a hidden love note in the form of an acrostic. This takes a little bit of time and thought, but can be a lot of fun. Clues to hidden gifts or the location for a rendezvous can also be hidden in an acrostic.

Magazine Messages

Using an underliner pen, go through a magazine and highlight words that end up saying your special message. Start at the front of the magazine and work to the back. Send your spouse the magazine in the mail or leave it on the seat of her car as an unusual love note.

The Personals

Run an ad unexpectedly in the personal column of your local newspaper. You can make the message overt or write it in code and give your mate a decipherer to figure it out.

Electronic I Love You

Punch into your spouse's home computer and write out a love letter in a file that he uses often. It will probably never be erased!

Insertion Cards

Many card stores or photo shops sell insertion cards: cards that allow a photo to be slipped into a slot. Have an accomplice take pictures of you, rush them through a one-hour developer, and send a card in the mail with your own message or invitation on the inside with your mug shot on the outside.

Collage Cards

Using construction paper, glue, felt pens, and photos cut out of magazines, create collage cards to send to your spouse. You can make them say anything you want and they can be wildly funny and personal at the same time.

Custom Mugs

Some silk screen or novelty shops offer custom-made messages on coffee mugs. Have one printed up especially for your spouse. For a real classy job, locate a potter and have him create a one-of-a-kind mug for your spouse.

Pinup Poster

Many photo stores offer poster-making services from standard photographs. Make a pinup of your spouse and hang it on the wall in the office.

Coupons

Create coupons that can be redeemed by your beloved at any time. For example, some may say "This entitles bearer to one free double-decker macadamia nut ice cream at 31 Flavors." Other possibilities: "A 30-minute backrub" or "I get up with the baby tonight."

Crossword Puzzle Message

Create a crossword puzzle love note using graph paper and a dictionary. This kind of love note can be great fun to decode as well as to read. Send it in the mail for your spouse to work on at lunchtime or break.

Picture Treasure Hunt

Create a treasure hunt for your mate. Decide where you will hide your treasure (this could be as simple as a nice meal at a fancy restaurant or a new diamond ring) and your "clues." Take your camera and photograph all of the places where the clues and treasure are to be hidden. (You may want to take a long shot and a close-up.)

Each day (or week, depending on how long you want to stretch things out) send your spouse a clue. At the location of the clue place the "long shot" of the next clue site. Your mate will then have to wait for the close-up photo to know the exact location of the next clue. (For example, the long shot may be of a corner park, the close-up may show the slide in the playground, meaning that the clue is taped underneath the slide somewhere.)

Be waiting at the treasure site with the last clue. (Hide in the bushes with a camera and film the reaction.)

ROMANCE

*The Romantic
Excitement
of Tradition
and Ritual*

REKINDLED

8

An often-overlooked but potentially exciting area of relationships comes with establishing and maintaining traditions or personal rituals by a couple.

The seasonal, monthly, or even weekly repetition of an event gives a sense of security and coherency to a relationship. It can become an extremely important point of reference to which all of life's other demands must stop and submit.

Traditions become the material that memories are built from. They give the warm glow of familiarity and remembrance each time they are celebrated.

Many traditions are passed down through families and find their way into the lives of a new couple. Often these traditions or rituals act as cement to weld two different backgrounds into one harmonious family. For this reason alone, they are a healthy addition to the lives of a couple.

Traditions and rituals are best started early in a relationship, but can be effectively instituted at any time in the life of a marriage. For example, one couple purchased their first Christmas tree six months after they were married. Both of them agreed that it would be more fun to decorate the tree with homemade ornaments than it would be to go and buy them at the store. This was the beginning of a long tradition. The tree was decorated a a bit thin the first year, but as Christmases rolled by, the tree filled up with various homemade ornaments. When children came, they too joined in the tradition started the first year of marriage by their parents.

Some traditions that start out as a romantic idea between spouses can keep that spirit and still absorb children as they come along.

Traditions do not have to be elaborate, only predictable. Most of the traditions couples celebrate together are hinged on a particular time of year or holiday. But any excuse is good enough to begin a tradition with.

Some traditions start from our desire to grow spiritually. A daily Scripture reading and prayer time together will strengthen your walk with God and deepen your love for each other.

Traditions and rituals can be a symbol... something that means "I love you" between two particular people. It can be a kind of flower, color, word, or code name.

The following ideas are traditions that other couples have built as part of their romance. Because a tradition is partly cultural, partly taste, and completely personal between two people, you may want to create your own list of traditions or even start some new ones!

SEASONAL TRADITIONS

Christmas is the most natural season for ritual and tradition because it comes already built in. Customize the holiday to fit your spouse. These ideas may really crank up the Christmas spirit.

Christmas Brunch

Have an annual Christmas Day brunch shared between you and your spouse. Make sure to purchase all of the supplies beforehand and have a leisurely late-morning meal. (This is especially good since kids will be busy with their toys.)

Worship Together

Attend a candlelight service together every year. Make it a tradition that lasts a lifetime.

Christmas Eve Special

Have a special gift set aside for your spouse to open on Christmas Eve (after the kids are asleep and the toys assembled). For example, you could make a tradition of buying your wife a very feminine piece of lingerie, her favorite perfume, or a special piece of jewelry each Christmas Eve.

Buy an Ornament a Year

Make it a tradition to go shopping for a new ornament

each year or buy one for the other person. At art fairs and some shops you can have special messages written on your ornament to make it more like a Christmas Valentine.

Make Your Own Wrapping Paper

Custom-make your own Christmas wrap each year. Use anything from rubber stamps to paint splatter, but make it a project between the two of you.

Christmas Bake Day

Working together, create delicious goodies to eat at home and to share with friends. Make sure to sit down and agree on what you will make, then go shopping together for the ingredients.

Christmas Tree Light Looking

Make a ritual of driving to look at the Christmas lights that decorate various parks, homes, or businesses. If you have the energy, make a tradition of creating your own Christmas display together. (Start out small by decorating a window or two. Who knows—in 20 years or so you may spread it down the whole block.)

New Year's Toss

Each New Year's Eve the two of you decide to get rid of something old and buy something new. You can make a ritual of dumping the old item in the trash or at the secondhand store and then buying the new item together.

Halloween Pumpkin Carving

Whether you have kids or not, it is still great fun to carve pumpkins together. If you live near a pumpkin patch, go out and select the gourd that best fits your personality, then each of you carve up a pumpkin. You may want to dry and save the seeds for snacks or buy a few more pumpkins and make a pie together. If you have children, you can even have a contest and give prizes for the most creative, the funniest, the most scary, the most realistic. Each pumpkin gets an award.

TRADITION AND RITUAL IDEAS FOR ALL OCCASIONS

Italian Night

One night a month go out for Italian food or pizza together. This could be set up as the second Tuesday in the month— or whatever you decide. This kind of tradition can include anyone who happens to be hanging out with you on the night you eat pizza. (If you hate Italian food or pizza, substitute any other food of your choice.)

Weekly Date Nite

Select one night a week and make it the night reserved for the two of you to go and do something special. If you have kids, make sure to reserve the baby-sitter on a regular basis.

A Special Flower

Select a special flower that is representative of your love for each other and try to give the flower as often as possible. Look for pictures that show it or stationery that has the flower on it. Pick the items up for your spouse or send messages using the symbol.

A Special Character

Select a special character that is a secret symbol of your love or of an event in your relationship. Try sticking this character in places where your beloved will get the message (kinda like the mark of Zorro). Put it in his lunch, on her pillow, or in an envelope sent to work or home (with nothing else in it).

The Special Show

Tune in one special radio show to which you both enjoy listening. Make it a custom to snuggle next to each other and enjoy the program. (Don't forget to unplug the phone so you won't be disturbed.)

Porch Swingers

Purchase a porch swing and as a couple sit out on the warm evenings of the year and watch the sun go down. Make it a habit for one night of the week.

Big-Deal Birthdays

Make a big deal about the birthday of your beloved. For example, you can make an agreement that he gets to do whatever he wants on his birthday and you will go along. You must watch and eat what he wants and listen to him tell you about anything he wants to talk about for the whole day. Of course, this works best if he plays by the same rules on your birthday.

Family Devotions

Pick a time each day to spend thinking about the Lord. Learn to pray together and share at least one thing that you are thankful for.

Saturday Morning Out

Start a tradition of breakfast together every Saturday morning. Let the kids fix their own cereal while you take a few hours at the beginning of the weekend together.

Camp Together

Make a tradition of camping together at a special time of year and perhaps always in the very same place. This is an inexpensive way to get off alone with each other.

ROMANCE

*Dating
Through
the Years*

REKINDLED

9

Have you noticed any changes in your marriage through the years? Marriages change and grow because of changes in the couple's circumstances and situations and their growing maturity. For example, a couple might start out surviving from paycheck to paycheck and in later years have an abundance of money in their savings account. Another common change is that most couples start out with no children but after a couple of visits from the stork the house is literally crawling with babies. Life is always changing and so we change with it.

We have identified in this chapter four major change points or milestones in the life cycle of a marriage. Each of these change points can affect dramatically the way the couple relates to each other romantically:

1. Newlyweds—Rookies of Love. These couples are married but really living the lifestyle of single people.

They are characterized as ambitious, impulsive, mobile, and flexible—the kind of people who might drive two-seat sports cars and spend weekends on the slopes.

2. Love and Diapers. The birth of children into the marriage relationship brings many new changes and adjustments (such as selling the sports car and buying a station wagon). This is the fast-paced world of babies, Little League, and car pools.

3. Still Crazy (About Each Other) After All These Years. Having adolescent children can bring some of life's greatest rewards and challenges to a couple. (Keep the station wagon, but buy extra sets of keys.) Parents with teens have more opportunity to do what they want to do because their children are more self-sufficient.

4. Alone Again—Whoopee! The parents are together again without children until the death of a spouse. (Sell the station wagon and the house and buy a motor home and a two-seater sports car.)

Let's consider what happens in each change point that keeps couples from enjoying romantic love and investigate ways to overcome those obstacles. We realize that the pressures and demands connected with each period of life can make it very difficult to continue the marriage, much less work on romancing your spouse. The feelings of romance in a typical couple's relationship have been crushed by a pile of concerns, insecurity, and a million things to do with no time to do them. However, we are convinced that no situation is too difficult to be overcome by a couple that wants to keep romance alive.

In some cases couples can even help each other to accomplish the goal of keeping romance in their lives. For example, a couple could work in cahoots with another couple to trade watching children on a particular night of the week so that both couples can have an evening to concentrate on their spouses only. For special occasions such as birthdays or anniversaries, a perfect gift might be to give another couple a night out complete with baby-sitting, a suggested romantic plan, money to pull it off, and the specific day it is to be redeemed. (Couples can make a habit of trading this kind of gift with each other on a regular basis.)

In the following pages you will find an in-depth look at the particular characteristics of each change point as it relates to romance in a marriage. We will also offer some potential dates and expressions of love that can fit the needs of couples in each category. (Many of the ideas can work for anybody, so read 'em all.)

NEWLYWEDS—ROOKIES OF LOVE

Being newly married is an exciting time of discovery when romance is at its highest. The honeymoon was wonderful and the new couple has moved into their home. Now the hard work of romance begins.

What has to be realized is that two very different people have been joined together. In a spiritual sense, God has made the two "one flesh," yet they are still individuals. They have much to discover about one another. In the process of living together as husband and wife, they will most likely find they have different habits that bug each other. He might snore at night while she has a habit of leaving her panty hose draped over the shower. He is a real night owl while she is alert in the morning. Their individual idiosyncrasies may take a bit of getting used to.

Often they will find that their expectations differ about marriage. The husband may expect that the wife's career will be less of a priority than his. The wife may expect that the husband will be home every night by 6:00. Who will initiate sex? Who will take care of the finances? Which set of in-laws will they visit during Christmas? The way the couple works through their expectations of one another will be critical to the future happiness of the marriage.

It is amazing how ill-prepared most people are when they enter into a marriage. Most individuals would not invest their life's savings into a project without carefully studying and researching everything they could so they were prepared for potential problems and knew what to expect. Most would not risk flying in an airplane if they were told their chance for survival was less than 50-50. Yet people get married every day with little or no preparation and with great odds against survival of the marriage. However, it is our contention that a couple's odds for survival are greatly increased if they work hard on their relationship. (The fact that you are reading this book is an indicator of promise for your marriage.)

In these first years traditions are started and precedents are established for the future. Put a priority upon your relationship. Continue to date like you did during your courtship. Don't let being too busy rob you of the joy of a romantic marriage. The investment you make in your relationship now will pay off in a big way later.

The following are some dates and expressions of love that can fit well in those first years of marriage B.C. (before children).

Celebrate the New House

Your first night in a new house (or apartment) can be an exciting and fun night for your romance. Push aside the boxes and get out the candles. (You may have to—the electricity may not be turned on yet.) Order take-out food and bring it back to your little hamlet. Dress up in your best clothes and make a special memory that you'll treasure for the years that you live there.

Decorate Together

Use some of the money that you received as a wedding gift to buy little decorations for your house. Plan together the style of home furnishings that you would like to aim for in your life together. Go through magazines and pick out the dream rooms. Shop together for things that will make your home "yours."

Start Traditions

See chapter 8 for lots of ideas.

Family Tree

Start work on a new family tree. Do it just for fun. Find as many photos of relatives as you can and make it a photo family tree.

Grazing

Visit a number of restaurants for appetizers or hors d'oeuvres only. Snack away and enjoy the environment and then move on to another restaurant for a whole different fare.

This can be a great source of fun and variety and a way to get a well-balanced meal at the same time.

LOVE AND DIAPERS

The addition of young children into the relationship has a significant impact upon the romantic life of a couple. Gone are the days when you could just pick up and leave on the spur of the moment or drop to the floor of your home in a fit of passion. With the addition of children comes a loss of privacy that will probably not be regained for the next couple of decades.

Along with the loss of privacy is a loss of intimacy. When a young mother has a new babe in her arms and a few other kids who seem surgically attached to her all day, even holding hands with her husband can be a real effort. You might hear her say in frustration, "There's just not enough of me to go around!"

A new father doesn't always understand his wife's predicament. All he knows is that his wife is not as interested in him as she once was. He might feel neglected, even a little jealous that the kids get all her attention.

When bedtime rolls around, the last thing on her mind is lovemaking. She doesn't feel sexy after a busy day with the kids—all she feels is tired. However, the husband needs the intimate touch of his wife. He needs a lover, not a mother . . . but the problem is she *feels* like a mother. She may be having a hard time losing those pounds added during pregnancy. Her self-concept is lowered. She may not feel sexy and therefore does not act sexy. Both partners are frustrated, and their romantic life is depreciated.

Parents with young children need to make time to talk to each other. Going out on a date once a week is crucial to the health of their relationship.

In order for this to happen, fathers need to be involved in affairs of the house. In fact a recent survey conducted with thousands of women indicated that this is the number one desire that women have of their husbands. Mothers have to feel that they are not leaving the house in chaos and the children not properly cared for.

For a man to walk into the house, announce that he is going to take his wife out tonight, and expect that she will drop whatever she is doing and take off with him is not fair. A myriad of things have to happen before the average mother feels she is ready to leave the house and kids. The wise husband will plan ahead, giving his wife some time to plan for the event herself. (You don't have to divulge the whole scheme for the evening, but you may want to give her hints as to the kind of clothes to wear and the time you expect her to be ready.)

However tied to the baby the new mother may feel, she must take time out to be a lover to her husband. Couples don't have to be gone for long or spend much money to make romance a meaningful part of their life. Just make it a regular part of the week. It may be helpful to find a night of the week to set aside as "date night." Finding a consistent baby-sitter is easier if that person knows that every Thursday night they'll be needed. They may view it more as a job and plan their week around it. Having a consistent sitter also brings more confidence and security to Mom so she can enjoy the time out.

Men need to get their wives out of the mother trap. And the trap only gets tighter as more children arrive. For many wives, it's still too hard to "leave the kids" when they do go out. They find themselves talking exclusively about the kids and not about each other.

Taking time for the intimacies of marriage gives a couple the opportunity to become lovers again. A healthy marriage is also the greatest gift that can be given to one's children. A creative, romantic life is a part of this healthy marriage.

The following list gives some great ideas to put spark back in a busy relationship.

The Care Package

During the week collect a number of small items that tell your beloved that he or she is special to you. These can be food items, things you make or bake, books, small items for an office, a picture of you or the family, or other favorite things that your mate might enjoy.

Box them all up with a love note and send them to your spouse at home or work. (Send the box by UPS or some other delivery service so that it is brought to the door.)

This surprise gesture of love can really make a day!

Do Disneyland Alone

Even though Disneyland (or any other theme park) is generally "kid heaven," it can be a lot of fun for adults too. Farm the kids out and enjoy a relaxing stroll through the shops on Main Street. Whatever you do, don't tell the kids where you are going or where you have been. You will have committed the unpardonable sin of "kiddom."

Nursing Mother Dates

A common problem for a new mother is that she can't leave the baby for more than a few hours because of the feeding schedule. However, the young couple still need time to talk, share their dreams, and enjoy being together.

One way to solve this problem is to work your dates around the baby's feeding times. Here are a few ideas for this special time in your relationship.

Candlelight Breakfast

Instead of the typical candlelight dinner, some couples find that a pre-dawn breakfast is just the thing. Set the mood as you would for dinner: cloth napkins and table covering, candles, china, etc. But instead of steak, serve omelets. Who knows—you might find time after the last feeding to be very romantic.

A Housekeeper (or Gardener) for the Day

A wonderful gift for a busy spouse is to surprise her with

the services of a housekeeper or gardener for a day. Make sure to prepare a card in advance (if the housekeeper can present it upon arrival, all the better). Make sure to inform the hired help to pay special attention to jobs that your mate may not enjoy or have the time to do.

Nanny for a Day

Instead of leaving your child for a day, bring a baby-sitter with you on an activity or date. Pay the sitter to occupy your baby and keep him warm, dry, and entertained. This can be a great method to almost get away from the responsibilities of parenting for a weekend.

Hour Dates

Create a list of things that both of you can do within the context of an hour. These do not have to be complicated—just times when you can be together minus baby. Obviously you will have to arrange for a sitter to stay with your baby or to drop Junior off at the home of a cooperative friend for the hour.

Some of the things that you could do together during this hour might include:

Sitting on the beach and soaking up the rays
Going out for appetizers at a local restaurant
Exercising together
Taking a bike ride through a park or along the promenade
Ice skating or roller skating

Bowling or playing miniature golf
Blasting golf balls at the driving range
Watching the sunset from the top of a building

STILL CRAZY (ABOUT EACH OTHER) AFTER ALL THESE YEARS

One of the greatest benefits this age group has is that the children are usually old enough to take care of themselves. Therefore, the spontaneity of earlier times can be renewed. If an opportunity for a fun time out presents itself, the couple can take advantage of it with a minimum of preparation.

Most couples in this stage have more time for each other but they also have more things competing for their attention. Being together is a choice that they make. It is saying to their spouse, "I love you and I want to grow old with you."

Another advantage these couples often have is money to spend on each other. Dinner out once a week is not a burden to them. Most have reached the peak of their earning power and can afford to treat each other to some luxuries.

Parents of teens have the time, the money, and even the desire to pursue romance, but in many cases it's been so long since they have initiated a date they have nearly forgotten how! What do you do? What do you talk about? Another problem may be that they have been doing the same thing for so long they have sensed a need for a change but don't know how to start. Here's where you ask your kids for help. Ask them what they do on a date. If it sounds like fun, then try it! You might even be able to talk them into double-dating with you (especially if you offer to pick up the tab). Don't be afraid to be adventurous and creative on your dates. You might have to modify what your kids tell you to fit your age and maturity, but we've found some great ideas come from the younger generation. By the way: You might need their cooperation and help to pull off some of your more creative dates.

Some couples who read this may say "We're just too busy to go out. Both of us get home around 7:00 exhausted from driving in freeway traffic only to find a dirty house, phone calls on the answering machine, and preparation that needs to be done for dinner."

It's easy to be so concerned with the practical concerns of life that we don't have the time (or desire) to think about romance. If their romance is to survive, couples must take time to think creatively about their relationship. Just the typical dinner and a movie may not suffice.

In an age of easy divorce, your model of a romantic, creative relationship will be an excellent example to your kids. You can also be assured that you will be an encouragement to your peers as well. It is often at this stage when many marriages sputter.

People around us desperately need models of romantic love. They will either get an unreal model from Hollywood or be privileged enough to see the real thing in you and your spouse.

The following is a list of ideas you might find helpful in romancing your spouse during teen years.

Hotel Room Rendezvous

Call your spouse at work and tell her to meet you at a certain hotel for lunch. Let her know you need her to arrange for an extended lunch time (i.e. noon to 3:00). After lunch take her to the room you have reserved. Since you paid for the room, you might want to return there later that evening and make a night of it.

Total Family Date

Involve your teenage kids in creating a date for your spouse. Have them act as butler and maid (rent uniforms if you can afford it) where they do the dishes, help with preparation and decor, or provide special music. You may need to tip these "employees" by offering them the car keys for the following evening.

Send 'em to Granny's

Pretend that you are newlyweds again by sending the kids to visit relatives (on the other side of the country) for a week. Relive the moments of spontaneous passion—and don't bother closing the bedroom door. Spend the week concentrating on each other. You can enjoy being away from your kids on occasion as much as they are sure to enjoy their adventures while away from you.

Love Travel

Go back to someplace where the two of you had a romantic experience in the past. Being in the same place you were many years ago and recounting the experience helps bring back the feelings that you may have forgotten. If possible, bring with you the music that was popular during that time and play it to set the mood.

If traveling with your kids, include them in a short sketch of your romantic history at the spot and put them up at another hotel while you enjoy a bit of the past and the future all at one time. (Kids are always surprised to learn that their parents once were gooey romantics and even used to kiss.)

Meet the Munsters

If your son or daughter is bringing a date by the house to meet you, secretly plan to dress up like the "munsters" or some other weird family (nerds, bums, socialites, bikers, etc.).

Surprise them both as you come out in costume. Then go out and celebrate your prank. (Hopefully you have raised children with a good sense of humor for this one.)

The Critics

Slip out and see one of the movies that your kids are bound to see BEFORE they do. (This should be the kind of movie that you would not normally go see yourself.) View the movie as critics. Over a meal begin to describe the movie like the critics do, and watch for the reaction of your kids.

ALONE AGAIN—WHOOPEE!

When the last child flutters out of the nest, a whole new world of excitement can open up to a couple.

Contrary to what is often depicted in the media, life does not end past 40 or 50. In fact many couples in the later age groups have a great deal of energy and vibrancy. And now they have the opportunity to once again invest it in each other!

Unlike the early years of marriage when the couple struggled to make ends meet, the years after the kids leave can find a couple with comfortable house payments (or none at all), few expenses, and expanded time to utilize!

This is a great time to rediscover each other. You both have changed since the early days of your marriage. You are wiser and probably much more insightful. You have a rich history of your times together in the past and a still-to-be-explored future.

A pair of lovers can refocus on demonstrating their love and thankfulness for one another.

Even couples in their later years can demonstrate that steady, warm flame of love for each other. Few things are more touching than to see a very old couple enjoying the company of each other. To see them happily driving their motor home down the road or peacefully sitting close to each other on a park bench brings a sense that this is "right," that this is the way it is supposed to be.

The following are a few dating ideas that might appeal to spouses who get to enjoy each other exclusively again.

A New Sport

As a couple, decide to take up a new sport. Consider swimming, para-sailing, windsurfing, or scuba diving (all which can be done with far less damage to your body than other sports but are still invigorating!)—or something active but nonaquatic such as badminton, croquet, or golf.

Spend the Kid's Inheritance

While your kids work for a living, take that cruise to the Bahamas you always thought about or even the slow boat to China.

The Bus to Nowhere

For a small bit of change the local bus system of many cities will take you to the end of the line. Make a day adventure of hopping off and on the bus (stopping to eat at any restaurant that looks good or at any shop that looks interesting) or hang out on the bus all day and see the sights (both inside and outside the bus). A real cheap thrill!

On Their Porch

If you have married kids, show up on their porch swing one night and make out. Give 'em a taste of their own medicine and have fun too. (If they don't have a porch swing, buy them one and show them what it is for.)

Skinny-Dip

You may have always talked about it, but now is the time to try it. Locate a private spot and splash around in the buff. (Night swims in a pool with the lights off can be loads of fun.)

The First Date...Revisited

Try and relive your first date together. Come as close as you can to duplicating it. If the place you went to is no longer in business, find someplace similar; if you brought flowers, do it again. If you sat in the car and talked, try doing the same.

Gone Fishing

Make a special adventure out of going trout fishing and then cook the fish on an open camp fire. Mmmmm good!

Jelly Making

Almost everybody loves the taste of homemade jams or jellies. Make a date out of picking fruit or berries and then creating homemade jam out of them.

Spinner Date

Draw a large circle on a piece of paper and write at various points of the circle the names of your spouse's favorite places to eat breakfast, lunch, dinner, or a snack. Using a small brad in the center of the circle and a paper arrow, create a spinner for your spouse to use in selecting where you will take her for a meal. (This is especially good when you are having a hard time deciding where to eat.)

Every State of the Union

Make it a goal to visit every state or province of your country. Try and eat dinner in each state capital.

Our House

Go back and try to find all of the homes you lived in as a couple. Take a picture of what each looks like now and compare it with what it looked like when you lived there.

My House

Go back and visit all of the homes you lived in as a child. Show your mate where you made forts and caught bugs. Walk through your old high school.

Take the Sleeper

Travel the country by train. Use the sleeper coach. Get off in small towns and spend time exploring them.

Grocery Race

The next time you go grocery shopping, divide the list of things to buy in half and have a contest to see who can get the items on the list and pass through the checkout stand first. Establish a penalty for the loser such as giving a five-minute scalp massage or washing dishes for a week. It's good fun and it gets the shopping done in a hurry. (For an added challenge, go to a supermarket with which both of you are unfamiliar.)

Meet You at the Tower

After the fall season many of the lifeguard towers at beaches and lakes are left abandoned until the next summer. These can make a great perch from which to view the sunset or to have a picnic out of the sand. Send your beloved a note telling her to meet you at tower number 4. Have a picnic all set up and ready to go. (Note: In some cases you may have to bring your own ladder to get up to the tower.)

Leaf Watching

Time a trip to get to the New England states in the fall. Rent a cottage and enjoy the leaves turning crimson and yellow.

ROMANCE

*Striking
the Match
of Romance*

REKINDLED

10

Every Boy Scout knows that a good fire is not started by dragging in huge logs of wood and trying to ignite them. The end result is a little smoke, lots of used matches, and frustration. They way to build a fire is to start small. Use dry kindling, bits of paper... things that are sure to take the applied flame. Gradually, larger pieces of wood can be added to the fire and they will catch because they have enough coals and heat to create combustion.

Igniting romance is very similar to building a great fire. Start small with the match of love.

Naturally, the degree of "small" or little gestures of love required may have a great deal to do with how cold the fire of our romantic love has grown. In some cases, it may take a great deal of "kindling" (or, in other words, layer after layer of consistently loving actions).

The small things that can help love to grow first start in our attitude. Being tender, good-humored, sympathetic, attentive, considerate, thoughtful, and helpful are good places to start.

Learning to tell our beloved how important he or she is to us is another vital piece of romance-building fuel. This can be done verbally or on paper . . . but it is essential that it be done. Look to God for wisdom, creativity, and imagination in how to love your spouse. He will be more than pleased to "direct your steps."

Just for a moment, think about your spouse. What are the qualities that you admire, respect, or are grateful for? What does he do well? What part of his or her physical body do you think is particularly attractive? If she were to die tomorrow, what would you miss most about her? What are the strengths of character he manifests? Make a mental note of those things or write them in the space provided below.

_____

_____

_____

_____

It is surprising the amount of things that we can find to love in our spouse if we stop and look for them. A good place to start building flames is to communicate in some fashion the attributes that you find delightful in your mate. Perhaps a love note or a whisper in the ear during a tender moment. Possibly a bouquet of flowers with a card that lists all the reasons you love her. (You could use a flower for each reason listed on the card.)

For love to leap into flames, we must tell our beloved

how we feel (unless we are sure that our spouse can read minds).

Another addition to stoke up the flames is overt thoughtfulness or doing something loving without the expectation of anything in return. It is the exercise of figuring out what would please our beloved and then doing those things. These do not have to be glamorous events, but they should be things that are above and beyond the various duties that we normally provide for each other. For example, most men come home from work each day empty-handed (except for a lunch pail or briefcase). To come home from work with a bundle of cut flowers or a small gift would be unique and special.

Take a few moments and think about special things that you could do for your spouse that would surprise, enhance, or please him or her. Write down your ideas in the space below (or someplace else) so that you don't forget.

_____

_____

_____

_____

_____

Make a point of doing as many of the things you have thought of as possible sometime within the next few weeks. Pick some to do this week. Pick one to do today!

Perhaps it has been months or even years since the two of you have done something special together without kids, friends, or relatives. Possibly there is someplace that

your spouse is always saying he would like to visit some-
day or perhaps some restaurant that she has always indicated she would like to try sometime. Now could be the
time for that special getaway date for just the two of you!
This could turn out to be not just a time to build up the fire
but to set off some fireworks as well.

Think of places that you know your spouse would like
to go (not where both of you would settle for, but specifically where your mate would enjoy). Use the space below
to jot down those ideas and to figure out how realistic it is
from the standpoint of budget, vacation time, etc.

_____

_____

_____

_____

_____

Special times away have to be created—they usually
don't happen automatically with most couples. Make sure
to put the relationship with your spouse above work,
sports, or friends.

The excitement of two people who work to keep romance alive is very contagious. It can spread like a benev-
olent flame to other couples who need to be "fired up."

Don't neglect to share with your friends any ideas that
have worked to bring you and your spouse closer together
and cause romance to rekindle. Every couple has to keep
vigilant over the romance in their life and contribute their
part to keep love blazing!

The dream of every couple who walks down the aisle on their wedding day is a future of love, appreciation, and romance. We hope that you will choose to keep that dream alive and that your life together can be one of laughter, gentle adventure, growth, and constant discovery of the person with whom you share a name, a bed, and the years. With a bit of effort and creativity from both of you, there is a good chance that your romance will never cool to ashes but will blaze brighter, deeper, and hotter with the kind of intensity that comes from a lifetime of being in love.

Other Good
Harvest House Reading

DATING YOUR MATE
by *Rick Bundschuh* and *Dave Gilbert*

If you've ever longed to return to those wonderful days of "courting," then *Dating Your Mate* is for you. Chock-full of clever ideas that will put the romance and excitement back in your marriage. A guide to creative fun for marrieds or yet-to-be-marrieds.

ROMANTIC LOVERS
The Intimate Marriage
by *David and Carole Hocking*

Here is romantic love for married couples that exceeds our greatest dreams and expectations! Greater intimacy is possible as we follow God's beautiful picture of marriage as found in the Song of Solomon.

GOOD MARRIAGES TAKE TIME
by *David Hocking*

Filled with teachings rooted in God's Word, this sensitive book offers help in four areas of married life: communication, sex, friends, and finances. Questions throughout the book for both husbands and wives to answer.

MARRIAGE PERSONALITIES
by *David Field*

Take a fresh look at marriage and its seven distinct personalities. Valuable information about marriage, new insights into your spouse's behavior, and an increased ability to give and receive deeper dimensions of love and joy.

THE INTIMATE HUSBAND
by *Richard Furman*

The Intimate Husband is the account of one man's decision to regain the love of his wife and save his faltering marriage. Talking with successful husbands around the country, he found the tools to reestablish the intimacy God intended.

FOREVER MY LOVE
by *Margaret Hardisty*

Selling well over 300,000 copies, this book has become an inspirational bestseller. Margaret Hardisty explains what a woman wants and needs from her man, and how very much she is willing and eager to give in return.

Dear Reader:

We would appreciate hearing from you regarding this Harvest House nonfiction book. It will enable us to continue to give you the best in Christian publishing.

1. What most influenced you to purchase *Romance Rekindled?*
   - ☐ Author
   - ☐ Subject matter
   - ☐ Backcover copy
   - ☐ Recommendations
   - ☐ Cover/Title
   - ☐ _____

2. Where did you purchase this book?
   - ☐ Christian bookstore
   - ☐ General bookstore
   - ☐ Other
   - ☐ Grocery store
   - ☐ Department store

3. Your overall rating of this book:
   ☐ Excellent   ☐ Very good   ☐ Good   ☐ Fair   ☐ Poor

4. How likely would you be to purchase other books by this author?
   - ☐ Very likely
   - ☐ Somewhat likely
   - ☐ Not very likely
   - ☐ Not at all

5. What types of books most interest you?
   (check all that apply)
   - ☐ Women's Books
   - ☐ Marriage Books
   - ☐ Current Issues
   - ☐ Self Help/Psychology
   - ☐ Bible Studies
   - ☐ Fiction
   - ☐ Biographies
   - ☐ Children's Books
   - ☐ Youth Books
   - ☐ Other _____

6. Please check the box next to your age group.
   - ☐ Under 18
   - ☐ 18-24
   - ☐ 25-34
   - ☐ 35-44
   - ☐ 45-54
   - ☐ 55 and over

Mail to: Editorial Director
Harvest House Publishers
1075 Arrowsmith
Eugene, OR 97402

Name _____

Address _____

City _____ State _____ Zip _____

Thank you for helping us to help you in future publications!